From the creator of Jonah and Arla's Light

Cradle in the Sky

A collection of hand written poems and a space for your thoughts from one grieving heart to another

EMMA ARMSTRONG

"A collection for the babies we never stopped loving, and the parents who never stopped feeling."

Dedication

*For the little lives who left too soon,
but left behind a love so vast,
it echoes through every heartbeat,
every breath,
every line of these pages.*

*To my own precious baby Jonah,
whose name is written in the stars—
you are the reason these words exist.*

*And to every grieving heart who picks up this book—
may you feel seen, held, and never alone.
This is for you.
This is for them.*

Introduction

This book was born from grief, but it is filled with love.

Every poem you'll find in these pages is a piece of my heart — written in the quiet moments of loss, the long nights of missing, and the soft whispers of memory. It's for the babies who are no longer here in our arms, but who live on in everything we do, in every breath we take, and every star we look up to.

Whether your loss was recent or years ago, whether you held your baby for a moment or only in your dreams — this space is for you. There is no timeline in grief. No right words. Just love. Just longing. Just connection.

You'll find poems here for memory boxes and robins, for missing milestones and chasing rainbows. For tiny sleepsuits that were never worn. For signs in the sky, feathers on the ground, and the ache that never quite fades.

This is not just a collection of poems — it's a place to rest. A place to remember. A place to feel less alone.

Thank you for being here.

With love,
Emma

You Are Not Alone

A note from one grieving heart to another

If you are holding this book, I know you carry a weight the world can't always see.
I wish you didn't need it.
I wish none of us did.

But since we're here—grieving, remembering, and loving in the quiet—I want you to know something:
You are not alone.

Your pain is valid.
Your love is endless.
And your baby, your child, your loss... still matters. Always.

This book isn't here to fix anything.
It's simply here to sit with you in the ache.
To give your heart a place to rest.
To remind you that someone else has felt this, too—and chose to write it down.

However you feel today, it's okay.
Whether you cry, smile, breathe deep, or simply turn the page...
you are doing enough.

And your love will never, ever be forgotten.

No Order, No Index

Because Grief Doesn't Follow Rules

*You won't find a table of contents here.
There is no index. No numbered journey.*

*Because grief doesn't move in straight lines.
It loops, it crashes, it disappears and returns without warning.
Some days bring peace.
Some bring tears from nowhere.
Some bring nothing at all.*

*And just like grief, this book is meant to be felt — not followed.
Open it at random.
Hold a page for days.
Skip ahead, then go back.*

*There's no "right way" to grieve,
and there's no "right way" to read this either.*

*Let your heart lead.
Let the poems meet you where you are.*

You are exactly where you need to be.

"Carried Still"

*I carried you quietly, heart to heart,
Whether days or weeks or a tiny new start.
You grew in my hopes, in dreams that I spun,
A whole little future that never got done.*

*You never took steps, or opened your eyes,
But you lived in the stars, in the deepest goodbyes.
No first word was spoken, no lullaby heard,
Yet your presence has echoed in every soft word.*

*The world may not see what I'll always know—
That love doesn't vanish, no matter how slow
Or short was your time, or unseen your face,
You left all your light in the quietest place.*

*So here I will hold you, where time cannot steal—
A child not forgotten,
A love I still feel.*

"I Never Got to Meet You"
from a sibling's heart

I never got to meet you,
But I know you were real.
You're part of all our stories,
And the way that Mummy feels.

They say you were so tiny,
Too perfect for this place.
But I still think about you—
Your name, your smile, your face.

I draw you in my pictures,
I whisper you goodnight.
You're somewhere in the stars now,
Or just beyond the light.

Some days I see Mum crying,
And Daddy's quiet too.
But we all still remember—
And we all still love you.

So even though you're not here,
You're part of all I do.
You're not just a memory...
You're still my sibling too.

"A Father's Grief"
for the baby I couldn't save

They said be strong, so I stayed still,
Held back the flood, against my will.
I carried boxes, made the calls—
While inside me, the silence falls.

I didn't hold you very long,
Not long enough to feel that bond.
But still, you live beneath my skin,
A quiet ache I hold within.

I watched her break, I tried to mend,
Played the role, became the friend.
But every night when lights go low,
I grieve the child I didn't know.

No tiny hand to hold in mine,
No lullabies, no borrowed time.
Just love that swells without a place,
And dreams of your imagined face.

So if I seem quiet, just understand—
I'm still your dad.
I still had plans.

"The Baby I Never Held"

I never heard your heartbeat sing,
Or watched the seasons that you'd bring.
But still, I dreamed of you each night,
A flicker small, a glowing light.

You came and went so silently,
A whisper on my history.
No crib to rock, no lullaby,
Just empty arms and asking "why?"

They say you weren't here very long,
But time can't measure love this strong.
You lived in me—in hope, in grace—
A soul that time could not erase.

Some won't see the tears I cry,
Or know I miss a little "why."
But I remember, soft and true—
The little life I never knew.

"Born Still, Loved Always"

I felt your kicks, your tiny dance,
I whispered dreams, I took the chance
To hope and plan, to picture days—
But fate would choose another way.

We dressed the room, we chose your name,
Not knowing things would not remain.
Your heartbeat stopped, the world went still,
And time stood quiet, against my will.

I held you close—so soft, so small,
A moment's peace, then lost it all.
You never cried or took a breath,
But filled the room with life and death.

They say you never lived at all—
But they weren't there to see me fall.
To feel your weight, to kiss your skin,
To say goodbye and tuck you in.

Stillborn, not unloved.
Brief, not erased.
You lived in my womb,
And still fill this space.

"For Tomorrow"

*I didn't know how I would make it here,
To a day called tomorrow without you near.
But somehow the sun still found my skin,
And the world kept turning, though you're not in.*

*Tomorrow once held dreams we planned,
Little shoes, soft hands in my hands.
Now it holds tears I didn't expect,
And memories I cradle so close to my chest.*

*But maybe tomorrow can hold love too—
A place where I carry the best of you.
A whisper of light, a quiet breath,
That says your story's not ended by death.*

*So I walk through the ache, step by step,
With sorrow behind and love that's left.
For though you're gone, you still remain—
In every soft tomorrow,
I'll speak your name.*

"A Grandparent's Grief"

*I was meant to hold your hand,
To watch you grow, to help you stand.
To spoil you with stories and soft embrace,
To see your smile light up your face.*

*But now I hold a different role,
With shattered dreams and aching soul.
I grieve for you, my darling one,
And for the parent—my own son.*

*I watched them break, I held them near,
I whispered love through silent tears.
For how do you fix what can't be mended,
When a tiny life has barely ended?*

*I never got to dry your eyes,
Or chase the clouds from lullaby skies.
But still you're part of all we do,
Forever ours, forever you.*

*You may be gone from time and space,
But always have a grandparent's place—
In quiet hearts, in names we say,
In love that will not fade away.*

"Broken, Not Imagined"
(for Broken Heart Syndrome)

It's not just in my mind, you see,
This ache that lives inside of me.
My heart, it cracked the day I knew—
The world would turn without you.

They call it syndrome, give it names,
As if that softens all the pain.
But science can't explain the sound
Of love collapsing to the ground.

My chest is tight, my breath is thin,
A storm of sorrow lives within.
And though you're gone, the weight you leave
Still grips my ribs when I can't breathe.

It's not just grief—it's something more,
A wound behind a beating door.
Not broken just from what I feel...
But proof that love can hurt so real.

"From a Friend Who Remembers"

I don't have the perfect phrase,
No magic words to heal these days.
But still, I sit beside your pain,
And whisper softly through the rain.

I saw your joy, I saw your fall,
I saw the silence take it all.
But through the loss, I've stayed right here—
To hold your hand, to wipe a tear.

I may not know the depth you feel,
But I believe your grief is real.
And in this space, I bring my heart—
A friend who won't let love depart.

I speak their name, I light a flame,
I honour both your joy and shame.
For though they're gone from sight and touch,
They mattered...
Oh, they mattered so much.

"I Am Still Your Mum"

I carried you beneath my heart,
And now I carry what's torn apart.
A lullaby I never sang,
A nursery quiet where silence rang.

They say in time the ache may fade,
But love like this was never made
To disappear or drift away—
You live in me, in every day.

I see your face in morning light,
I whisper your name into the night.
Though arms are empty, soul is not,
You're every breath this world forgot.

I wear a smile that hides the storm,
I move through life, a different form.
But underneath, my truth stays true—
I am still your mum.
And I always will be, too.

"The Shape of You"

There's a space where you should be,
In the everyday, invisibly.
A gap in all our ordinary things—
Your laugh, your tears, your growing wings.

The toys are still, the clothes untouched,
The air too quiet, far too much.
And though the world moves on outside,
A part of me remains inside.

I see your shadow in the light,
I dream of you most every night.
And in the wind, I hear your name,
It softens me, then breaks the same.

You are not gone in how I feel—
Your absence makes your love more real.
I live each day with missing you...
Still loving all the shape of you.

"You Were Here"

You never took a single step,
Or spoke a word I'd hear...
But every inch of me still knows:
You were here.

You never saw the morning sun,
Or felt the passing year...
But time still bends around the truth:
You were here.

I felt your flutter, soft and small,
Then faced my greatest fear.
But no amount of silence dims
That you were here.

A name, a love, a whispered light—
Not gone, just changed, my dear.
You live in me, in all I do,
Forever near.
Forever clear.
You were here.

"More Than One Goodbye"
For the loss of multiples

We dreamed in twos, or threes, or more,
Tiny heartbeats we adored.
A nursery full, our arms so wide—
Yet grief came in and stepped inside.

We counted kicks and made our plans,
Imagined life with holding hands.
But fate was cruel, and time stood still,
Now quiet cradles barely fill.

One goodbye is hard to bear,
But more than one feels stripped and bare.
A love divided, yet still whole,
Each little name etched on my soul.

I light one candle, then one more,
Each flame a star I now adore.
They came with hope, they left with grace,
And still, I feel them in this space.

Don't ask me how I carry on—
With pieces missing, yet love so strong.
I mother them with silent tears,
Through empty arms and aching years.

So if you see me glance above,
Know my heart is full of love—
For not just one, but more I miss,
Each one a memory, each one a kiss.

"Born, and Loved, and Gone Too Soon"
For neonatal loss

You came into this world so small,
A fleeting breath, a fragile call.
We held you close, we kissed your face,
In that short time, you filled all space.

The monitors, the quiet hum,
A fight for life had just begun.
And though your stay was far too brief,
You left behind a world of grief.

Ten tiny fingers, perfect toes,
A love so fierce, it only grows.
Your name is whispered in the breeze,
Your memory lives in quiet seas.

We bathed you in our hopes and prayers,
Wrapped you gently, eased your cares.
And when it came to say goodbye,
We held you close and let hearts cry.

You were our dawn, our brightest light,
You made the darkest hours bright.
Though life was short, your mark is deep—
You are the love we always keep.

"The Wait"
For those walking the road of fertility

I build a cradle in my mind,
Soft blankets folded, dreams aligned.
Each month, I open hope again,
And close it gently with the pain.

The world moves on, and still I wait,
At every door, at every gate.
A name I've never spoken yet,
Already stitched inside my chest.

I smile through showers, cards, and cheer,
And hold my aching heart so near.
For every "maybe" turns to "no,"
And still I plant, and still I sow.

There is no marker, none can see
This quiet war that lives in me.
But in the silence, love still grows—
In empty rooms, my spirit knows.

I carry hope like fragile glass,
With every cycle that must pass.
A love not yet placed in my arms,
But always waiting, always warm.

"Behind the Smile"
For mental health and holding on

Some days I wake and breathe on cue,
But feel the weight of pushing through.
A thousand thoughts I cannot tame,
And yet I show up just the same.

You see a smile, a laugh, a glow,
But not the storms that ebb and flow.
The sleepless nights, the silent screams,
The hope that hides in broken dreams.

It's not a fight with swords or flame,
But with the shadows, guilt, and shame.
A quiet war inside my mind,
Where peace is something hard to find.

But still I try—each breath, a win,
A promise to not cave within.
I'm not "just sad," or "overly blue"—
It's real, it's raw, it's pulling through.

So if I say, "I'm fine," today,
Please know I mean, "I'm finding a way."
And if you're walking through this too,
I see you. I believe in you.

"When I Look at the Stars"
For those we miss beyond this world

When I look at the stars, I feel you near,
A silent whisper I still hear.
Not in words, but in the light,
That dances softly through the night.

Each star a story, each one a flame,
And somehow, each one knows your name.
They shimmer like the love I keep,
The kind that lingers, strong and deep.

The sky becomes a gentle sea,
Of all the things you'll always be—
A light, a hope, a guiding part,
That fills the quiet of my heart.

I talk to you in breathless skies,
And trace your shape with weary eyes.
You're not so far, not gone, not lost—
Just past the veil, beyond the frost.

So when the night is dark and wide,
I let the stars stand by my side.
And in their glow, I find the grace
Of all the ways you still have place.

"Chasing Rainbows"
For the hope after the storm

They say a rainbow follows rain,
But mine was born from silent pain.
A dream I held with trembling hands,
That slipped like water through the sands.

I chase the colours through the grey,
With aching steps and words I pray.
Each streak of light, a whispered name,
Each hope I hold, never the same.

Not every rainbow comes with sun,
Not every journey feels like one.
Sometimes it's tears that paint the skies,
And love that teaches how hope flies.

I chase, not just for joy alone,
But for the ones I've always known.
The ones I carried, loved, and lost—
The ones who live beyond the frost.

So when you see me look above,
Or speak of faith, or endless love,
Know I am chasing more than hue—
I chase the dream of holding you.

"Carrying You, Carrying Them"
For pregnancy after loss

This isn't just a second chance,
Or turning page in life's advance.
It's joy and sorrow, hand in hand,
Two beating hearts—one barely stands.

You grow beneath my careful skin,
While memories stir deep within.
A baby gone, a baby here—
Both held so close, both held so dear.

Some days I smile, some days I cry,
Some nights I simply wonder why.
But still I love with all I am,
Both for the now and for the then.

You are not here to replace the one—
The star I lost, the missing sun.
You are a light, a life anew,
And still I carry all of you.

So if I pause, or breathe in deep,
Or speak to ones I couldn't keep—
Know every moment, raw or bright,
Is laced with grief and bound in light.

"Light in the Dark"
For when you're finding your way

There are days the dark feels endless,
Like night has swallowed day,
When hope is just a whisper
That flickers far away.

But even in the silence,
When you feel you've lost your spark,
Your soul remembers how to shine—
There is still light in the dark.

It may be soft and hidden,
Not the blaze you had before,
But even gentle embers
Can guide you to the shore.

A hand you held, a voice you knew,
A love that still remains—
They're stars that live inside you,
Still shining through the pain.

So take your time and breathe again,
Let healing make its mark.
You are not alone, dear one—
There is still light in the dark.

"Whisper in the Wind"
For those we still hear, though they're gone

You're not so far, not gone for good,
Though life moved on as if it could.
I feel you near in ways so small,
A brush of breeze, a distant call.

You're the whisper in the wind,
That finds me when the day grows thin.
A voice not heard by any ear,
But in my heart, you're always near.

No need for words, no need for sound,
Your love is where the hush is found.
In rustling trees and skies that bend—
You come to me, my silent friend.

You speak in moments I can't see,
But still, you find your way to me.
A presence soft, a love so kind—
A whisper only grief can find.

So when the wind begins to blow,
I close my eyes—because I know.
It's you, it's you, again, again...
A whisper carried by the wind.

"Nightmare"
For the grief that doesn't sleep

I didn't wake from this nightmare—
It followed me into the light.
Eyes open, heart still screaming,
Nothing about this feels right.

It wasn't just a dream I had,
It was the day my world stood still.
And now the nights are haunted
By the love I couldn't fill.

I reach for you in shadows,
But find the empty air.
Your name becomes a whisper
That echoes everywhere.

I cry in silent corners,
I break in bathroom stalls,
Because this nightmare walks beside me,
In shops, in streets, in calls.

They say it fades, or softens—
But I'm still gasping for my breath.
Some nights I sleep beside my grief,
Some nights I sleep with death.

But I rise because I must do,
Though nothing feels the same.
And even in this nightmare,
I still speak your name.

"The World Moves On"
For the quiet grief no one sees

The world moves on, it always does,
With busy streets and needless buzz.
The clocks still tick, the traffic hums,
While silence wraps around my lungs.

I see the smiles, the passing days,
The changing seasons in their blaze.
But time stands still inside my chest,
Where memories refuse to rest.

They ask less now, or not at all,
As if my grief should somehow fall.
But love like this—it doesn't fade,
It doesn't leave, it's only made.

The world moves on, but I remain,
A little softer from the pain.
A little slower, deep in thought—
For all I had, and all I lost.

I walk this path, unseen, alone,
A different heart than I was shown.
But still I love, and still I stay—
For them, I carry on each day.

"Spring"
For hearts learning to breathe again

The earth begins to wake once more,
Soft blossoms bloom where cold once tore.
The skies grow wide, the winds grow kind,
But still, you linger in my mind.

The birds return with songs to sing,
And yet, I ache for everything.
The daffodils, in golden rows,
Can't fill the space where sorrow grows.

But spring is not a cure for pain,
It's just a hand through quiet rain.
A breath, a bud, a promise made—
That beauty can still touch the shade.

So let the petals fall and rise,
Let light return to tired skies.
I'll walk this season tenderly,
With grief, with hope, and memory.

"Summer"
For grief that lingers in the light

The sun is high, the skies are blue,
The world wears gold in every hue.
And still, my heart walks tender ground,
Where echoes of your name resound.

Laughter floats on warmer air,
But not all hearts are light in there.
For mine still aches, though flowers bloom,
And every breeze still sweeps your room.

The days are long, the nights are sweet,
But grief and warmth so often meet.
A memory in each setting sun,
A whispered thought of what's begun—

And what was lost along the way,
The things I'd planned, the words I'd say.
But still I stand beneath this sky,
And let the summer soften why.

You're in the shimmer on the sea,
In sunbeams gently touching me.
Not gone—not really, not too far...
Still glowing where the wild things are.

"Autumn"
For the season of remembering

The leaves let go without a sound,
A golden hush upon the ground.
And in their fall, I see my own—
The things I've held, the love I've known.

The world turns soft in amber light,
A fading warmth, a coming night.
And though the breeze begins to chill,
Your memory holds my heartbeat still.

There's beauty in the slow decline,
In every tree, a secret sign.
That letting go is not the end,
But part of how the branches bend.

I walk through woods in quiet grace,
Still looking for your little face.
And find you in the rustling air—
The way the earth begins to care.

So let the autumn skies turn grey,
I'll love you through each fading day.
And know that loss, though sharp and deep,
Is where your soul and mine still meet.

"Winter"
For the cold seasons of the soul

The world is wrapped in quiet white,
A hush beneath the pale blue light.
The trees stand bare, the sky hangs low,
And still, I carry all I know.

Your name, like frost, clings to my skin,
A warmth I hold so deep within.
Though days are short and nights are long,
Your love remains, still just as strong.

Winter does not ask for cheer,
It holds the space for every tear.
A time for hearts to pause and break,
To feel the ache that others fake.

But even here, where silence grows,
Where bitter winds and sorrow flows—
There is a beauty, still and true,
In all the ways I carry you.

The snow may fall, the fire may fade,
But love like ours cannot be swayed.
So through this frost, I walk and yearn—
For spring to come... and your return.

"All Your Firsts"
For the moments we never got to share

I dreamed of all your firsts, my love—
Your first sweet smile, your steps above.
The way you'd call my name one day,
The games you'd laugh at when you'd play.

Your first warm bath, your first soft shoes,
The bedtime books, the morning news.
Your tiny hands, your wobbly walk,
Your baby babble, toddler talk.

I pictured birthdays, candles bright,
And cuddles through a stormy night.
First day at school, a painted card,
A fridge of scribbles, love unmarred.

But those firsts never came for you—
They vanished like the morning dew.
And now I hold, so tight, so dear,
The firsts I never got this year.

Your first hello became goodbye,
Yet still I see you in the sky.
And though you're far from where I stand,
Your firsts still live within my hands.

Each one a wish, a breath, a start—
Forever etched upon my heart.
I carry them, though we're apart...
All your firsts, inside my heart.

"My Boy"
For a son forever loved

My boy, my heart, my sweetest name,
The world without you isn't the same.
I held you close, I kissed your skin,
And wished for time to just begin.

Your fingers curled around my own,
A fleeting touch, and then... alone.
But not in love—you're held so tight,
In every shadow, every light.

I speak to you in silent ways,
In midnight tears and empty days.
I see you in the softest skies,
In stars that shine with quiet eyes.

My boy, you were my every dream,
Now stitched into each moonbeam.
I carry you through all I do—
The part of me that still is you.

No length of time, no stretch of space,
Could dim your light, erase your place.
My arms may ache, my voice may break,
But oh, my boy, you're mine to take—

In every heartbeat, every sigh,
In every whispered lullaby.
You are my always, my forever joy,
My little love... my darling boy.

"My Girl"
For a daughter held in the heart

My girl, my light, my gentle grace,
I see you in each quiet place.
In petals soft, in skies that blush,
In every still and sacred hush.

I dreamed of braids and tiny shoes,
Of bedtime songs and morning news.
Of giggles spilled across the floor,
Of kisses pressed behind a door.

But fate had other plans for you,
And left me with a love so true—
That even death can't steal away
The bond we made that precious day.

My arms still reach, though they are bare,
My soul still finds you everywhere.
In every breeze, in every star,
My girl, you're never truly far.

You were the hope I longed to meet,
A lullaby so soft, so sweet.
And though this world was not your stay,
You left your light to guide my way.

My darling girl, you'll always be
The strongest thread that runs through me.
Not just a loss, not just a part—
You are my whole, my beating heart.

"Those Unnamed"
For the babies known only by love

No name upon a paper line,
No whispered call at sleeping time.
No birthday cake, no printed card—
Yet still, your absence hits so hard.

You never wore a knitted hat,
Or felt the weight of this or that.
But still, you lived within my soul,
A dream that made my spirit whole.

They never knew your tiny face,
But in my heart, you held your place.
A flicker, soft, a sacred spark—
A light that vanished in the dark.

Unnamed, but never unloved, dear—
I speak to you though no one hears.
A silent bond, too deep to say,
That lives in me each passing day.

You are the tears I cry alone,
The ache beneath my every tone.
Not just a wish, not just a thought—
But someone real, so gently caught.

So here's to you, the ones we miss,
Who never felt the world like this.
No name was given, yet still you stay...
Forever in our hearts, always.

"Time Is a Thief"
For the love that outlives the moment

Time is a thief, it comes so fast,
It takes the now, and makes it past.
It stole the cries I longed to hear,
The milestones we held close and dear.

It slipped between the waiting hours,
It withered dreams like fading flowers.
No warning bell, no chance to hold—
Just moments lost, and silence cold.

I blinked, and you were out of sight,
A shadow lost to morning light.
No lullabies, no future plans,
Just folded clothes and empty hands.

They say that time will help me heal,
But time can't touch the love I feel.
It only stretches out the ache,
And adds up all it couldn't make.

But even thieves can't steal it all—
The way I loved, the rise, the fall.
Your name, your place, your gentle spark,
Still live in me beyond the dark.

So take your time, but know this truth—
My heart still beats with all your youth.
You may have slipped through time's cruel hands,
But love—our love—forever stands.

"Sunset"
For endings that come too soon

The sky turns soft, the light grows low,
And once again, I feel you go.
A hush falls over land and sea—
The sunset brings you back to me.

Not in the way I longed to keep,
But in the silence, broad and deep.
In golden streaks across the sky,
I hear your name, I breathe a sigh.

The day is done, the light must fade,
But still your memory's gently laid—
In every hue, in every glow,
In all the places love can go.

They call it ending, drawing near,
But I see beauty through my tears.
For though the sun slips out of view,
It always leaves a trace of you.

So when the world turns dusk and wide,
I sit and watch with arms open wide.
And somewhere in that final light...
I hold you close, and say goodnight.

"Goodnight, My Angel"
For the one I carry in my heart

Goodnight, my angel, soft and small,
The brightest soul I ever saw.
The stars now hold your gentle light,
And I still whisper love each night.

I tuck you in with silent hands,
In dreams that drift like seaside sands.
No lullaby, no cradle near,
But still, I feel you resting here.

I would have rocked you night and day,
Sung every fear and ache away.
But heaven called too soon, too fast,
And left me holding what can't last.

Still, every night I close my eyes,
And find you there beneath the skies.
Your spirit wrapped in moonbeam glow,
A love too deep to let me go.

So goodnight now, my darling one,
Though life and time have come undone.
You're in my heart, you always will—
My angel baby, sleeping still.

"Forever"
For love that doesn't end

They say that time will help me mend,
That sorrow fades around the bend.
But love like this—it doesn't die,
It doesn't drift, it doesn't lie.

You're in my breath, my every sigh,
The tear I wipe, the reason why.
You may be gone from touch and sight,
But still you glow in every light.

Not just a moment, not a phase,
You live within my endless days.
A part of me, beneath my skin—
Forever where you've always been.

No measure holds this kind of love,
No ending line, no push, no shove.
It simply is—a quiet flame,
That flickers softly with your name.

So even as the world turns fast,
And people say "move on, it's past,"
I'll carry you, both near and true...
Forever starts and ends with you.

"Our Love"
For the bond that nothing can break

Our love was written in the stars,
Before this world could leave its scars.
A quiet thread, so strong, so true—
Forever binding me to you.

It bloomed before your first small breath,
And held its shape beyond your death.
No time, no space, no final day
Could ever take that love away.

It's in the way I speak your name,
In tears that fall without a flame.
In every dawn, in every night,
Our love still burns, a steady light.

They may not see, they may not know,
But through my soul, you softly glow.
Not gone, not lost, not out of view—
My heart still beats because of you.

So when the world forgets your face,
I'll hold you in our sacred place.
Where love is louder than the pain...
And I would choose it all again.

"Clouds"
For the ones we miss in every sky

I look up at the clouds each day,
And wonder if you passed that way.
A wisp of white, a drifting line—
A sky that feels a bit like mine.

They float so soft, they move so slow,
Like all the love I'll never show.
No footprints left upon the land,
But you are there, just out of hand.

A blanket stretched across the blue,
A silent space that carries you.
And when the sunlight pours right through,
It feels a little more like you.

I watch the sky in quiet thought,
For all the joy and time we ought.
Yet somehow in the air above,
I feel your peace, I feel your love.

So if you ask me where you are,
I'll point beyond the furthest star.
But also to the clouds that stay—
Still holding you, just miles away.

"I See You Everywhere"
For the love that lingers in every place

I see you in the morning light,
In skies that turn from dark to bright.
In drifting leaves and dancing air,
My love—you're truly everywhere.

You're in the song the robin sings,
In whispered winds and silver wings.
In flowers blooming soft and slow,
In every place I chance to go.

I see you in the passing rain,
In echoes only hearts explain.
In shadows cast by candle's flame,
The world still softly speaks your name.

I see you when I'm all alone,
In quiet corners I have known.
And even when the room feels bare,
I close my eyes... you're always there.

You never left, not really gone,
Your presence in the dusk and dawn.
Though I can't hold you, still you stay—
In everything I see each day.

"White Feathers and Robins"
For the signs that say you're near

A white feather falls without a sound,
No footsteps heard, no one around.
And yet I know it's more than air—
It's you, reminding me you're there.

A robin lands so still, so near,
A flash of red, a feeling clear.
They say you come in wings and song,
To show me love still lingers strong.

No words are said, no hand to hold,
But in these moments, I feel bold.
As if the veil is thin and wide,
And you are walking by my side.

A feather on a windowsill,
A robin when the world is still—
These signs, they help my heart believe
That though you left, you didn't leave.

So when I see those wings take flight,
Or find a feather soft and white,
I smile and send a whisper low:
I miss you more than you could know.

"Sleepsuit"
For the outfit never outgrown

Folded neat in a quiet drawer,
A tiny suit you'll wear no more.
The tags still on, the seams still clean,
A memory of what might have been.

I held it up against my chest,
Imagined how you'd look your best.
Soft cotton made for dreams and rest,
Now clings to grief I can't digest.

No midnight cries, no sleepy yawn,
No morning stretch to greet the dawn.
Just threads and buttons left behind,
And love that time could never unwind.

I press it close some days, and cry—
It smells of hope I can't deny.
A little piece of what we planned,
Still waiting for your tiny hand.

Sleepsuits shouldn't stay so new,
But this one holds the heart of you.
And though you never wore it long,
In it, your memory stays strong.

"Memory Box"
For the treasures of a life too short

It isn't full of toys or noise,
No cluttered books or baby joys.
Just little things, so soft, so small—
Yet somehow, they contain it all.

A lock of hair, a name so sweet,
A card, a tag, a tiny sheet.
A bracelet with a number worn,
The only things you ever "wore."

Each piece a story left untold,
Each fold a memory I hold.
Your weightless things are heavy still—
Because they show the love we feel.

I open it with gentle hands,
And let my heart revisit plans.
It hurts, it helps—it's all I've got,
A box of love that time forgot.

It shouldn't be this way, I know,
But here your presence seems to glow.
And though you're gone, this space is true—
It holds the best of me and you.

"It's Not Goodbye"
For when love goes beyond this life

It's not goodbye, not really gone—
You're with me still, you linger on.
In every breath, in every sigh,
I feel your love, I don't ask why.

The world may turn, and time may pass,
But still I see you in the glass.
A glance, a light, a scent, a song—
It's how I know you're not so long.

I said goodbye with breaking heart,
But you and I will never part.
You're stitched into my every day,
In all I do, in all I say.

So when they say you're far from here,
I smile through one more falling tear.
Because I know the sweetest truth:
You're in my soul, you are my proof.

It's not goodbye, just see you then—
I'll hold you in my arms again.
Until that day, I'll carry you,
In everything I love and do.

Now, Your Voice

From words you've read... to the ones you hold inside

You've walked through poems shaped by love, by grief, by memory.
You've turned pages filled with heartache, with hope, with longing.
And now, this space is for you.

These next pages are not about perfect words.
They're about your voice.
Your story.
Your quiet moments.
Your tears that no one sees.
Your love that never left.

Let this part of the book be a soft place to land.
A journal. A letter. A whisper. A scream.
Whatever you need it to be.

There is no pressure here.
Only room for you — and the one you miss.

A Letter to My Baby

A space to say what's in your heart

There are so many things I wish I could say...
So I'll write them here.
Words of love. Words of longing.
Things I never got to say out loud,
and things I whisper in the quiet.

Write as little or as much as you need.
There is no wrong way to grieve — only your way.

Dear my sweet baby,

....
....
....
....
....
....
....
....

With all my love, always,

....

A Letter to My Baby

Dear my sweet baby,

....
....
....
....
....
....
....
....

With all my love, always,

....

Things I Wish I Could Tell You

*There are words that stayed inside me.
Moments I never got to say out loud.
This page is for those thoughts—unfinished, unspoken, or still unfolding.*

*You can come back here again and again.
Write them in love, in longing, in your own time.*

I wish I could tell you...

....
....
....
....
....
....

The Signs I See That Remind Me of You

*Some say it's coincidence.
But I know it's you.
In feathers, robins, stars, and sudden songs—
You find your way back to me.*

*Use this page to write the signs that bring you comfort.
Let it be your quiet collection of moments that feel like a whisper from beyond.*

These are the signs that remind me of you...

....
....
....
....
....

What Hope Looks Like Now

*Hope doesn't always look like it used to.
Sometimes it's tiny. Sometimes it's distant.
But it's still there, even in the gentlest forms.*

*Write what hope looks or feels like to you now—
even if it's soft, quiet, or still growing.*

Hope looks like...

....
....
....
....
....

Today I Remember...

*For the memory that rose unexpectedly.
For the moment that pulled on your heart.
For whatever it is you carry today.*

Write it here—just as it is.

....
....
....
....
....
....
....
....

A Quiet Moment

*Sometimes grief is loud.
And sometimes, it's silent.
This page is for the hush—the stillness between the tears, the thoughts, the love.*

....
....
....
....
....
....
....
....

What My Heart Needed to Say

There are no rules here.
Only space for whatever needs to come through—grief, love,
longing, anger, peace.
Let your heart speak, and know it's safe here.

....
....
....
....
....
....
....
....

A Moment I'll Never Forget

There are some moments we carry forever.
A glance. A sound. A feeling.
A second when time stood still.

Use this page to write the memory that returns again and again.
It may hurt, or it may comfort — or both. Let it be what it is.

I'll never forget...

....
....
....
....
....

You Lived. You Mattered.

Even if the world didn't see.
Even if time was too short.
You were here. You are loved. You matter.

Use this space to honour your baby's presence, no matter how brief.
Write about who they were to you, and who they will always be.

You were...

....
....
....
....
....

The Words I Needed to Hear

*Sometimes it's not what people said—
It's what they didn't say.
Or what we wished someone had said.*

*Use this page to write the words your heart longed for.
The kindness, the honesty, the truth that grief deserved.*

I needed someone to say...

....
....
....
....
....

Where I Feel You Now

Grief changes—but love remains.
Sometimes, we feel them in small, sacred places.
In a room, a sky, a smell, a memory.

This page is for those quiet connections.
Where your baby still feels close.

I feel you when...

....
....
....
....
....

If You Had Stayed

Sometimes the hardest part is wondering who they might have been—
How they'd look, what they'd love, how they'd laugh.

This page is for the daydreams.
It's okay to imagine. It's okay to miss what never had the chance to grow.

If you had stayed, I think...

....
....
....
....
....

The Item I Treasure Most

Grief lives in the smallest things.
A blanket. A bracelet. A photograph. A sleepsuit never worn.
It's not just an item — it's a part of your story.

Use this page to write about the object that holds the most meaning.
Why you keep it. What it means. Why it matters.

I treasure this because...

....
....
....
....
....

A Message From Me to You

This is a space to speak freely —
From a parent's heart to a baby's soul.

Whether it's a message of love, apology, gratitude, or simply I miss you,
let your words be what they need to be. There is no right or wrong here.

From me to you...

....
....
....
....
....

The Life I Carry Now

Grief doesn't leave,
but life begins to gently grow around it.

This page is for the life you're living now —
with them in your heart, in your steps, in your every breath.

Here's what life looks like now, with you still part of me...

....
....
....
....
....

Light a Candle, Speak Their Name

This page is a quiet ritual.

Choose a time. Light a candle.
Speak their name aloud. Speak it softly, or say it in your heart.
Let this be your moment—just you and them, wrapped in light.

Date: ....
What I felt or remembered in that moment:
....
....
....

Draw Your Rainbow

*Sometimes, hope shows up in colour.
This page is for your rainbow—whether it's the child that followed,
the light you found again, or the dream that still lives in your heart.*

*Use this space to draw or write your rainbow.
You can use colours, shapes, words, or simply mark it with your heart.*

Feather Messages

*Feathers are often signs from those we miss.
This page is for messages carried by air—words you'd like to
send into the sky.*

*Write a message on a feather. Draw it, imagine it, or simply
close your eyes and speak it aloud.*

If I could send you this today, it would say...

....
....
....
....

67

My Symbol of You

*Every grieving heart carries a symbol—
a star, a flower, a colour, a name.
Something that means them. Something you see and just know.*

*Use this page to draw, write about, or describe the symbol that
reminds you of your baby.*

*Your symbol is...
And to me, it means...*

....
....
....

Envelope of Wishes

*Imagine an envelope addressed to the stars.
Inside: your wishes, your dreams, your love.*

*Use this space to write what you would place inside—
and know that love always finds its way.*

If I could send you these wishes, they would be...

....
....
....
....
....

Poetry & Journaling

A space for your heart to feel and your hands to rest

*This book is more than just poetry.
It's a place to write, to remember, and to gently honour
all that love leaves behind.*

*Some pages will hold words I've written — pieces of
grief, of longing, of memory and hope.
Others are left for you — soft, quiet spaces for your own
thoughts, stories, tears, or silence.*

*You don't need to fill every line.
You don't need to follow a path.
You can simply let this book hold what you're not ready
to say aloud.*

*Whether you come here in stillness or storm,
may you find comfort in both the poetry...
and the space between.*

Closing Words

For wherever you go from here

*If you've read, written, cried, or simply held this book in your hands,
thank you for letting it be part of your journey.*

*Grief is not something to finish.
It's something you learn to carry,
to live beside,
to honour in your own quiet way.*

*Whether you filled every page or just a few,
whether you return to this often or rarely—
please know that every part of your love still matters.
Your baby matters.
Your story matters.
You matter.*

*This book doesn't close the story—
but it closes with love.
Always.*

*With you in memory,
With you in hope,
With you in heart.*

You are not alone.

This book was created from love, loss, and the quiet spaces in between.
For every grieving heart who needed somewhere to go, for every parent who carries their child in memory instead of arms—
this is for you.

May the words within these pages sit beside you in the silence.
May the journaling offer you space to breathe, remember, and hold close what never fades.

Your love is forever.
Your grief is valid.
Your story is seen.

Thank you for letting this book be part of yours.

Printed in Dunstable, United Kingdom